T0209822

TOOLS
FOR
RECOVERY

Diane Deeley RN, C.A.R.N.

Editor: Jeanette Whitbeck, MS

BALBOA.
PRESS

A DIVISION OF HAY HOUSE

Balboa Press books may be ordered through booksellers or by contacting:

Balboa Press
A Division of Hay House
1663 Liberty Drive
Bloomington, IN 47403
www.balboapress.com
1 (877) 407-4847

Print information available on the last page.

ISBN: 978-1-9822-1671-9 (sc)
ISBN: 978-1-9822-1669-6 (hc)
ISBN: 978-1-9822-1670-2 (e)

Library of Congress Control Number: 2018913934

Balboa Press rev. date: 12/04/2019

DEDICATION

Dedicated to my husband Joe who always encouraged me to step out of my comfort zone and live out my dreams.

CONTENTS

Foreword..ix

What is Addiction?...1
What is a Higher Power?.................................9
Twelve Steps..11
Choices 23
Communication 31
Unforgiving 39
React vs. Respond..51
Wilderness Journey 55
Setting Boundaries 61
Co-Dependence 63
Dysfunctional Families..................................67
Withdrawal 71
How to Spot a Relapse...................................75
Building Your Supports..................................85
Word for Family and Friends.........................89

FOREWORD

When I first started working in the field of addictions 28 years ago, I had no idea how life changing it would be. I had an absurd idea that if I explained things clearly and engaged the clients, they would respond and change what they needed to change. I look back and realize that I probably changed more than anyone else. Over the next three years, I learned more and more about addictions. In addition, I finished all the classes and the exam to become a Certified Addictions Registered Nurse, C.A.R.N.

As a Registered Nurse, I understood the physical side of addictions, but had a lot to learn about the psychological and spiritual part. It is not just learning about how addictions affect the body, it is taking an entirely different approach to making changes when every inch of your body is resisting that change.

I have watched people come into treatment and despite everyone betting against their success, they have done amazingly well and have long years of sobriety. I have also seen people constantly relapse or lose their life to the addiction. They are really trying, but continue to relapse.

Is it that some are ready to change, or could it be they are surrounded by the right people at the right moment in their life? Maybe, for whatever reason, they make real changes in their body, mind and spirit. I am always delighted to hear from someone who is doing well and I also accept the fact that not everyone will be able to do it today. Apples ripen on different days and people don't arrive at the same destination the same day.

You have to learn skills to cope in the world without a drink or drug. Part of the problem is you may have started to use substances at a young age (teenage years). Once you learned to use a drink or drug as a way to cope, you didn't have to go through the normal angst of learning social skills for dealing with your peers and family. However, you will need many of these skills for the rest of your life. For example:

- Building relationships
- Dealing with hurts
- Being reliable
- Improving communication
- Making better choices
- Asking for help

The problem is if you start getting sober at 20, 30, 40, 50, or whatever your age, you may still have some coping skills of a 14 year old. It will take time and practice to improve those skills.

I learned one thing that keeps me coming back every week to teach the classes. *I cannot get anyone sober, but if I can give one person a tool they can use when they are ready, it is worth it.*

One thing I honestly believe is that right now everyone has inside them all the things they need to move their life in a positive direction. It is not dependent on when everything gets better in your life. There will always be issues with health, relationships, jobs, other people, anger, betrayals, financial, and a million other reasons to put off making changes.

Addiction is not about bad people.

It is about a bad disease. I believe that people with addictions are very sensitive to the world and have to learn skills to cope without a drink or drug.

You have to remember that we all learn a little differently and not at the same pace. This book contains some of the classes I have taught for the last 28 years. These are the ones that many people have said influenced them the most.

The following chapters are tools that I share during the classes. These tools are suggestions on how to improve your life. It is just like riding a bicycle. You must practice and practice until you can ride it with ease.

My hope is this book helps you in your journey towards recovery.

WHAT IS ADDICTION?

When we talk about addictions, people want to know:

- What is addiction?
- What causes addiction?
- What are the different kinds of addictions?

Let's start with: WHAT IS ADDICTION?

- Is it the drink or drug you use?
- Is it how often you use? Is it daily use, once a week, binging on weekends?
- Are you addicted if you still function fairly well with work and family, still have a license, look good, have a job and fine things?

My definition is:

It is causing problems in your life and you can't stop

It doesn't matter what you are addicted to. It could be any drink, drug or behavior that causes a problem for you or people in your life. You feel as if you can't live without it. It has become your best friend and lover, covering up insecurities and fears, relaxing you and protecting you from uncomfortable feelings. It takes away all problems (for the moment).

Many of you feel that it is a problem for other people, but not you. You spend a lot of energy convincing yourself that you can control it WHEN and IF you decide to stop. You know you have a strong will and have been successful in other ways despite your use.

Some of you look at people who are living on the street, unkempt and hungry and think that is what addiction looks like. The reality is that these people are only a very small percentage of those with addictions.

If you think none of this applies to you, be brave and ask people in your life whose opinions you value. See if they have observed any problems with your behaviors. Many of you aren't aware of the chaos you are causing.

WHAT CAUSES ADDICTIONS?

- Environment?
- Psychological?
- Physical?
- Emotional?

- Bad Childhood?
- Abuse?
- Heredity?

All of the above may be part of the reason you turned to addictive behavior, however, it does not affect everyone that way. Some people may experience a combination of these causes and have no problems with addictions. Others can't track their addiction back to anything or anyone in their background. And some are addicted as soon as they "touch" any mind-altering chemicals (alcohol or drugs).

One man told the class that he has been addicted to alcohol for over 30 years. He remembered how amazing he felt the very first time he tasted alcohol. He was five years old and at a party for his parents. He took a sip of peoples' drinks. Everyone thought it was cute. He started sneaking alcohol after that and never stopped.

Others said they used a variety of substances when they were younger, but didn't develop the ADDICTION (can't stop) until they used a certain drink or drug and they lost all control. That can be a different substance for everyone.

Currently, there is a growing Opioid/Heroin epidemic that is claiming an alarming number of lives due to over-doses. Some addictions may start after being given pain medications (opioids) following surgery, dental work, broken bones or for chronic pain management. This has also become more common in the over 55 age group due to injuries and falls. You believe you will stop when you no longer have pain, but find that your body has quickly become ADDICTED physically and mentally to the opioids. You are unable to stop using due to the severe withdrawal symptoms that last for several weeks. You are now desperate to relieve your withdrawal symptoms.

After a while the doctors can no longer write you more prescriptions for the original pain medications, and you cannot function without them. When you can no longer get your pain pills legally, you turn to Heroin which gives you the same feeling. You don't realize the ADDICTION has taken over your life. You require more and more drugs to satisfy your body's craving.

Unfortunately, Heroin can have other substances added to it. Fentanyl, one of those substances, depresses respiration and has been a major cause of heroin over-doses and deaths.

WHAT ARE THE DIFFERENT KINDS OF ADDICTIONS?

SUBSTANCE ABUSER:

Some people use the same amount of drink or drug that you use, or even more, but with enough motivation can walk away from it.

You realized that you couldn't have all the things you want in life (family, good job, self-respect, and freedom) if you continued to use. Some of you have serious health issues that

4

are threatening your life. You stop drinking or drugging, and make needed changes. You have ABUSED a substance but were able to stop. You were able to make the necessary changes to get your life back on track.

Remember: it is not the amount or frequency that determines if you are ADDICTED. It is the inability to STOP despite mounting problems in your life.

A good example of people who ABUSE a substance are teenagers. All their friends are doing it. Many can walk away as they get jobs, families, and other responsibilities. Unfortunately, many get stuck in powerful addictive behaviors.

DRY DRUNK:

You stop using and have long periods of abstinence, but you continue to take your frustration out at work or on family and are difficult to be around.

You make some changes in your behaviors and life may improve (if only because you remember where you left your car or still have a car) but YOU ARE NOT ENJOYING YOUR LIFE.

Something is missing. You feel inadequate without your drug of choice. Blaming others for being unhappy becomes a way of life. You are difficult to live with and express a lot of negativity. You are very prone to relapse.

Diane Deeley RN, C.A.R.N.

SOBER:

You decide there is NO CHOICE except to get sober. You are WILLING TO DO WHATEVER IT TAKES. You take suggestions and DO THE WORK.

It is very hard for you to look at yourself and find serious changes are needed. You are not sure you can or even want to change and don't know where to start. You know deep in your bones that if you don't stop, you will end up in jail or dead. It is time to ask for help. You use all the tools you are given and develop a sober support network of people who understand what you are going through. It is a total commitment that takes complete honesty with yourself and others.

As you make the journey of Recovery, you become happier and willing to help others who are afraid to commit to sobriety.

In the past 28 years, I have had the pleasure of hearing from people who have totally turned their lives around and became the fine people they were meant to be. It is not an easy journey, but very rewarding as they discover a new purpose. They have learned so much and are willing to step up and help someone else find their way.

STORIES SOMETIMES MAKE IT CLEARER.

We had a 42-year-old woman come into the rehab from the intensive care unit at the hospital. She had severe Cirrhosis of the liver from alcoholism. Cirrhosis is a scarring of the liver and those areas of the liver no longer function. Unfortunately, hers was very severe and her liver was barely functioning. She had an enlarged belly, swelling of her legs, shortness of breath, and yellow skin and eyes. She needed many naps due to her frail condition. I was not sure she was getting much from her rehab experience.

Fast forward four years. A woman approached me one day and asked if I remembered who she was. I had no idea. She had beautiful long brown hair and was wearing a stunning white suit. She introduced herself and told me who she was and reminded me about her journey with addiction. I was amazed. She appeared healthy, with no signs of any illness. She looked radiant.

I asked her how she was and she explained that when she left rehab she never touched another drink. This changed her life. She told me she became involved in AA and developed a sober group of friends. Despite being told that she may not recover, her health has continued to improve and she feels healthy again.

I think it is important to know that no one has all the answers or knows what the future holds. It was a clear message to me that anything is possible when you are willing to try.

WHAT IS A HIGHER POWER?

When I talk in class about a Higher Power, eyes roll and people slump in their chairs. Some would disconnect from the conversation. I don't think it was because they didn't care. More likely they were confused, hurt, angry, felt left out, or felt unworthy. They struggled with the concept of a Higher Power.

People have been arguing over what a Higher Power means for centuries. I don't think we can give an answer in just a few words. It's something we don't fully understand.

So the very basic idea is WE together have a HIGHER POWER than I alone. If that is the only concept you can hold onto at this moment, that's okay. WE can help each other.

There are many religions in this world. There is good and bad in all religions because people are involved and truly believe their path is the best. Religion is a way many people find their Higher Power/Spirituality. Unfortunately, disagreements over which Religion is right and which one is wrong have caused wars for thousands of years.

Higher Powers are called different names: God, Jehovah, Allah, Yahweh, Christ, The Divine, Supreme Being, The Universe, and Nature. These are just a few.

I do believe there is a Power greater than me, and I continue to ask for help. I don't think any of us have it all right. I do think that this HIGHER POWER is available if you ask.

Learning to TRUST is very hard. If you have issues with trust due to past behavior of others or yourself, it is a big leap to say or think about trusting something you can't see or touch.

Reaching out and asking for help from your Higher Power is a big step in letting go. When I am at a loss as to what I should do and ask for help, I am always amazed at how someone shows up or something happens that provides some guidance. I also know that when I try to make all my own decisions without asking for help, my frustration rises and things don't improve.

The gift of addiction is learning that you are NOT the most powerful force in the universe and you don't have to do it by yourself. There is plenty of help, if you ask.

A simple prayer is: PLEASE HELP ME.

TWELVE STEPS

1. We admitted we were powerless over alcohol—that our lives had become unmanageable.

2. Came to believe that a Power greater than ourselves could restore us to sanity.

3. Made a decision to turn our will and our lives over to the care of God as we understood Him.

4. Made a searching and fearless moral inventory of ourselves.

5. Admitted to God, to ourselves, and to another human being the exact nature of our wrongs.

6. Were entirely ready to have God remove all these defects of character.

7. Humbly asked Him to remove our shortcomings.

8. Made a list of all persons we had harmed, and became willing to make amends to them all.

9. Made direct amends to such people wherever possible, except when to do so would injure them or others.

10. Continued to take personal inventory and when we were wrong promptly admitted it.

11. Sought through prayer and meditation to improve our conscious contact with God as we understood Him, praying only for knowledge of His will for us and the power to carry that out.

12. Having had a spiritual awakening as the result of these steps, we tried to carry this message to alcoholics, and to practice these principles in all our affairs.

Living the Twelve Steps

The Twelve Steps are an excellent way to help make changes in your life. It is not the only way, but if you don't have a solid plan, it is a very powerful one. They give a clear roadmap that will lead you to a better life. The Steps are not something that you do once and are done. Rather, they are something that you use over and over to keep you safe and heading in the right direction on your journey.

You will find that you will need to revisit each step many times and not always in the same order. They will help you find your Higher Power and tap into help. They will give you clear instructions on how to clean up your behaviors and become a person of character. They also call you to reach out to other people who are struggling with addiction. Part of working the program of recovery is reaching out to others. You can never forget that you can't do it by yourself. One powerful phrase that is often used is:

You can't keep it if you don't give it away.

Step One

We admit we are powerless over alcohol/drugs and our lives have become unmanageable.

Many don't believe you are POWERLESS. You still feel that you can stop if you want to, despite losing your family, possessions, health, or job. Imagine yourself in the back of a police car in handcuffs. They are all terrifying feelings when you have no control over the outcomes. If your life is going well, you have no reason to change anything.

Until you acknowledge that you are powerless over your addiction, you will not change. Some of you may be afraid you can't find a way out, so you don't try. You lost so much you feel hopeless. Are you holding onto fears, resentments, or other reasons, and using them as an excuse to not change?

What does UNMANAGEABLE mean? What is going on in your life that isn't working? How do you give yourself permission to continue a negative behavior?

Have you ever tried to change your drug of choice and hope you have fewer problems? What about using excuses? I worked all week and I deserve this. I still look good, and haven't lost everything. We all want to be in control, but being honest, willing, and open are essential for recovery.

Step Two

Came to believe that a power greater than ourselves could restore us to sanity.

Some of you don't believe there is a power greater than yourself. Maybe you always had to rely on yourself for safety or things have happened in your life that made you distrustful and afraid.

Many think that a BELIEF system only means RELIGION. People have different RELIGIOUS beliefs and, amazingly, when you compare them they have great similarities. They teach love and kindness and a belief in a Higher Power, even if that Higher Power has different names: God, Jehovah, Allah, Christ, Yahweh, Divine, Supreme Being, The Universe, and Nature. These are just a few.

If a group teaches exclusion, hate or judgmental thinking, that is not from a Higher Power but from people adding their own opinion. Some believe their way is the only correct way.

Each of us is made up of a BODY, a MIND, and a SPIRIT that connects us with the world. RELIGION is a way of looking for SPIRITUALITY.

Where do you find this Higher Power? Listen to people who have a peacefulness and purpose about them. They are not just talking the talk, but walking the walk. They work the steps and their lives are proof that it works. Taking suggestions is a good way to start looking for your Higher Power.

A Higher Power works through people and puts them in our path when we need them. Reach out to positive people.

Step Three

Make a decision to turn our will and our lives over to the care of God as we understand him.

How do we do that? Some people are still struggling to understand this idea of a Higher Power. Let me ask you: What would happen if someone comes in this room and I am alone and he/she has the intention of hurting me? What are my chances? Probably not good. Now what if someone comes in the same room with the intent of hurting me and ALL of you are here? My chances are probably much improved!

WE together have a Higher Power than I alone. Taking suggestions is a great start.

For example, when there is a fire, the firemen tell you to stop, drop, and roll.

When you need help try pray, say, and do.

Pray is simply asking for help.

Say is speaking positive words.

Do is doing the right thing even when no one is looking.

At meetings you may hear the first three steps referred to as:

- I can't
- He can
- I think I'll ask

Step Four

Make a searching and fearless moral inventory of ourselves.

Think about cleaning out your garage or storage area. You have to take everything out. Then you have to clean out the cobwebs and trash and see what's there. Next is to decide what needs to get thrown away, what needs to stay, and what needs to be repaired before it is useful. It's not all bad stuff.

We have good in us that we don't want to lose. Spend some time looking at the good in yourself. You will find things that you really like and some things you have to change. You can't work on fixing your life until you clean it up and see what is causing problems.

Looking at yourself and finding faults is difficult for everyone.

Suggestion: Do **4th step** work when you are safe and have had a clear head for a while. If you do it too soon with no support, it may be too upsetting. You may not have enough tools to help you do it safely. Having a sponsor to support you is a good idea.

Step Five

Admit to God, to ourselves, and to another human being the exact nature of our wrongs.

Why should we tell God or anyone?

Remember, WORDS ARE CONTAINERS OF POWER. Holding onto guilt and shame keeps you stuck. Once you tell someone, it relieves you of the burden of carrying it alone. It also frees you to make needed changes. You can't fix something until you know it is broken.

Step Six

Were entirely ready to have God remove all these defects of character.

Are you ready to give up some behaviors that have been beneficial in protecting your drink/drug use? Things like manipulating, lying, putting your needs first? What do you have to change? Everything that brings you back to your ADDICTION. Are you willing to do the work? No one is going to do it for you.

If you're feeling you want to change but not sure you can, go back to Steps One, Two, and Three. Remind yourself that there is help from a Higher Power along with people you reach out to.

It's the unknown that's scary. You have to trust that if you do the work, your life will change. It's a step of HOPE.

Step Seven

Humbly ask Him to remove our shortcomings.

What is the difference between Step Six and Step Seven? Seven is the ACTION Step. Step Six is getting ready and Step Seven is committing to it. Doing things differently even if it is uncomfortable.

Everyone has faults, but it's important to identify the behaviors that keep protecting your ADDICTION. Start with them.

When we are humble, we admit our way isn't working and we need help. You will learn to trust that your Higher Power will help you when you can't do it alone. Pay attention to the people who come into your life with words that encourage you. The more you make small positive changes, the easier it is to make bigger ones.

Step Eight

Make a list of all persons we have harmed and become willing to make amends to them all.

This is not about beating yourself up. We all have good and bad in us. This is an opportunity to be honest.

Sometimes it is impossible to undo something without causing more harm to others. You can't make amends, but it is a big step to owning your behaviors.

Step Nine

Make direct amends to such people wherever possible, except when to do so would injure them or others.

This is the ACTION step that follows Step Eight. First we get ready and then we take action. Start doing and saying the right things and eventually it will get more comfortable.

Sometimes we can't make amends directly because people are no longer alive or do not want you in their life. Offering a sincere apology is a good way to start, if possible. It makes you responsible and frees you from carrying negative baggage the rest of your life.

How many times have you said "I'm sorry" and then continue with the same behaviors? Cleaning up your act will cause others to judge you. Be prepared for that. Not everyone is ready for you to change. They have learned to live with your negative behaviors and when you change, it affects them too. Rebuilding trust will be an issue. Expect it.

These middle Steps (Four, Five, Six, Seven, Eight, and Nine) are all about making changes. They aren't always done in order or neatly. Life can be messy. Go back to Steps One, Two, and Three to build your confidence.

Step Ten

Continue to take a personal inventory and when we are wrong we promptly admit it.

What is the difference between Step Four and Step Ten? Step Four is getting rid of old baggage and Step Ten is all about being honest on a daily basis. It is all about RIGOROUS HONESTY. You need to do it EVERY DAY. It is the step that prevents RELAPSE. If you start being dishonest with yourself, you are headed for trouble. Our PRIDE gets in our way in life. No one enjoys being wrong.

DO THE RIGHT THING WHEN NO ONE IS LOOKING.

Pick up after yourself. Pay your bills, do your fair share, and give an honest day's work. Confront your mistakes and apologize even if it is embarrassing. Everyday, take a minute to see how you are doing. We all need to improve. You may not be where you need to be, but Thank God, you are not where you used to be.

It's much easier to correct small things rather than wait until we have a whole garage full of junk built up and no clue where to start.

Step Eleven
Sought through prayer and meditation to improve our conscious contact with God, as we understand Him, praying only for knowledge of His will for us and the power to carry it out.

If you have never prayed, how do you do it?

Do you only pray when you need something? It doesn't have to be long and complicated. "HELP" is a great prayer. "SHOW ME WHAT TO DO AND HOW TO DO IT" also works.

How do you MEDITATE?

If you know how to worry, you know how to meditate. It's just focusing on being peaceful instead of on the negative. If you want to change, you have to look for new tools and practice them. If you want to learn anything, you have to spend the time learning it. You had to learn many skills in life, like riding a bike, tying your shoes, reading, texting. They all took time and effort to get comfortable. If you want to learn to meditate, spend five minutes a day paying attention to ONE thing around you.

Step Twelve

Having had a spiritual awakening as the result of these steps, we tried to carry this message to alcoholics/ addicts, and to practice these principles in all our affairs.

What does our spiritual awakening mean? It may be a little different for everyone. It is a change in your attitude. It gives you the freedom to realize that you are not in control and helps you accept suggestions.

One part of Step Twelve is sharing what you have learned to help others. We all have special talents and abilities that we need to share. If you want a good, happy life, get up every morning and decide to help someone. Being a positive role model may change your life along with many others.

If you are tired of meetings, go anyway to encourage others. Make a point of sitting next to someone who looks uncomfortable. No one can do this program alone. As you help others, you help yourself. Remember the saying:

You can't keep it if you don't give it away.

A **GPS** guides you one street at a time, even if it is a long journey. The **TWELVE STEPS** guide you one day at a time.

The Steps are a road map. They will be a guide to a new, better life. YOU have to work them. No one can do it for you.

CHOICES

We have many choices to make in life and sometimes we don't even realize it. It's not the BIG choices that we don't recognize, it's all the little ones that just seem to happen on their own. In recovery, it's important to pay attention to all the little choices.

If you keep ending up with a mess in your life, it's time to look at the patterns that are not working.

What do you **HEAR**?

Most of us don't realize that 80% of what we hear is what we tell ourselves.

- I can't
- I'm not good enough
- It's too hard
- I'm so bored
- I'm smarter than everyone, so they can't help me

Think about what you're telling yourself. Did those thoughts come from you or did someone tell you those things? Can you remember what someone said to you that changed the way you think about yourself?

- I expect good things from you
- You are such a caring person
- You have so many talents
- You are pretty, handsome, or smart

OR

- Your father was no good and you are just like him
- You never get anything right
- You are not smart enough

Now take a moment and think about a teacher, coach, or family member and a real memory you have. Did it make you smile or feel bad about yourself? WORDS ARE TREMENDOUS CONTAINERS OF POWER that can hurt as well as heal.

What we **HEAR** is what we **THINK.**

That's good when it helps us make good choices, but not good when our thinking leads to a bad outcome.

BE CAREFUL WHO YOU HANG OUT WITH. Are you surrounding yourself with people who give you permission to lower your standards? Do you hang out with people who drink or drug? You tell yourself it is okay because you are not using, or it's just this once. You haven't seen your friends in a while and miss them. You are heading down a slippery slope. Do you think you are entitled? You worked hard and the weekend is here. BIG CAUSE OF RELAPSE. Entitlement is a killer.

What we **THINK** is what we **SAY**.

Remember WORDS ARE CONTAINERS OF POWER. We have a much better chance of making better choices if we **SAY** it out loud.

Today, I will:

- Not smoke
- Be more honest
- Make no negative comments
- Give a compliment

We all have a lot of things to improve in our lives, but people tend to get overwhelmed. It may help to pick ONE behavior to work on, and do that one thing until it improves. My favorite is swearing. It is amazing how hard that is, but the outcome is remarkable! You may not realize how much you swear and how it affects you and people around you. Who it attracts into your life. You need to get honest with yourself and make your own list.

What we **SAY** is what we **DO**

The more you **SAY** and **DO** the right thing, the better you get at it and the more comfortable you become. If you just think about it, it probably won't happen.

If you tell people what you will **DO**, you are more likely to **DO** it. It's important to **SAY** what we are going to **DO** and tell people. That way you feel obligated to actually **DO** it.

Sometimes it is hard to change direction, but **DOING** it is the start of a new life.

What you **DO** becomes your **HABIT.**

HABITS are not formed overnight. When you were young and learning to ride a bike, you may have fallen and skinned a knee. But you didn't give up. You got back on the bike and practiced it over and over again until you could ride without even thinking about it. It takes the same amount of practice to learn a new **HABIT**.

The first part is **SAY** what it is and owning it. Then you have to **DO** the right thing over and over until it becomes a **HABIT**. It gets easier over time.

You may be thinking that you cannot change everything. You don't have to. You just have to change the things that are destroying your quality of life and preventing you from being the best version of yourself. You change your life by changing **HABITS**.

"Habit is habit, and not be flung out a window by any man, but coaxed downstairs going one step at a time."

Mark Twain

HABITS become your **CHARACTER**

When you always do the right thing, even when no one is looking, it says a lot about who you are. It develops your **CHARACTER** muscles. After a while you won't even stop to think about what choice to make. Your **CHARACTER** knows. It's like riding that bike. You don't have to tell people that you are a person with **CHARACTER**. They see it.

Think about when you started first grade. You knew after the first week of school which kids were smart, kind, funny, mean, or a bully. Who you liked and disliked. You figured it out without anyone telling you.

Your **CHARACTER** becomes your **DESTINY**.

If you are a person of **CHARACTER**, you will have a better **DESTINY** because you are on the right path, even when life throws you a curve ball. It doesn't guarantee that you will have a perfect life. It just helps you play the game of life with a clear head.

If you keep finding yourself in bad situations (no job, family problems, multiple rehabs, or repeated problems with drinking or drugs) and think it is just bad luck, take a better look.

The best way to change a bad **DESTINY** is to go back and see where you went off the path. Let's work backwards to see what is not working.

If your **DESTINY** isn't taking you where you want to go, then look at your **CHARACTER**. If you have lost your values and convinced yourself that you are entitled to be dishonest or unreliable or…whatever your story, then look back at your:

HABITS. Are you reliable and trustworthy, working regularly, paying your bills. If not, look at what you are:

DOING. What are you filling your days with? Are you working on leaving old behaviors behind and developing new ways to deal with life? What are you:

SAYING. Are you back to saying it is really not that bad; recovery is too hard; everyone is so tough on me; I can't do this; or lying, swearing, etc.? Did it start with what you were:

THINKING. Do you **THINK**:

- I just have to do it my way
- I'm going to change, but not today
- This is way too hard
- Recovery is too boring

Maybe your thinking is way off the mark because of what you:

HEAR. What are you telling yourself with self-chatter? Are you back hanging out with the people, places, and things that convince you that you are fine? Life will be boring if you give up your drugs or alcohol?

Take an HONEST look at where you went off the path and then climb back on the bike and start the ride again.

UNTIL YOU LET GO, YOU WILL NEVER CHANGE WHAT YOU HOLD ON TO SO TIGHTLY.

COMMUNICATION

It's all about communication. You are a social being and need contact with others. That's the hard part. You need to become more aware of how to improve your ability to communicate.

When you first start to make changes in recovery, you may realize that your communication with family and friends needs to improve. It is a very difficult time for everyone.

When I asked people how many ways they could communicate, they gave these examples:

- Facial expressions
- Verbally
- Body language
- Eye rolling
- Singing
- Sign language
- Dance

- Art
- Shutting people out

Most of the time, you communicate a lot about yourself before you open your mouth.

When someone speaks our language, we respond.

If I stood up and spoke for an hour in a different language than yours, after a short time no one would pay attention.

Let me share a story about communication. When I was in Senegal, West Africa, working on a medical mission, the local language was "Woolof" and I communicated thru translators. I had learned some very basic words in that language, but was hardly proficient. I was in a small, remote village with 90 villagers, no running water or outhouses.

One evening I took a walk around the village and passed a small one-room cinderblock house with a thatched roof, dirt floor, and a curtain covering the doorway. There was a black pot sitting on a fire outside the door.

A woman appeared and waved her hand for me to enter her home. Pointing to myself, I questioned ME? She pulled open the curtain and I entered.

We communicated with smiles, hand gestures, and body language. She told me she had three babies, who were sleeping behind a curtain inside her home. She did this by holding up three fingers, acted as if she was rocking a baby, and then tilted her head to the side onto her hands as if she was sleeping. She pulled the curtain aside to let me see her babies on blankets.

I used similar gestures to let her know that I also had three children. The rest of the time she showed me how she did her needle work, what she was cooking in the black pot, and her other crafts. We had a cup of tea cooked over a fire. We had a wonderful time with only a few words spoken. I realized how much we could communicate. When I returned to my group, they wanted to know how we talked. I told them that we both spoke a common language called "MOM".

I left the village realizing that PEOPLE ARE MORE ALIKE THAN DIFFERENT, and if we want to communicate, we have to look for a common ground to start.

Unexpected kindness is the most powerful and underrated agent of human change. I was a stranger and she was so kind and welcoming to me. If we want to improve relationships, we must start by being the agent of change.

Many times we wait for someone else to change before we make changes to improve a relationship. In truth, we must take full responsibility for our own actions and how they affect others. Being nice and treating someone with respect, even if you don't feel like it or don't think they deserve it, is where you start.

It may not sound fair, but we are not worried about fair. We are trying to rebuild a relationship that is broken and needs help. You may have played a part in why it broke down in the first place.

To repair broken relationships, you have to make changes in YOUR behavior to show another person they are important to you. Here are five behaviors that your loved ones may want from you. We all notice behaviors from others that make us feel loved. They are different for all of us. Here are five of the most common ones.

1. **TOUCH**: Being intimate, holding hands, sitting close to them, touching, and hugging are just a few ways that you show you care. Most children really feel loved with touch. Some people just naturally feel comfortable reaching out to greet people with a hug. Being physically close or holding hands is very natural for many. If that behavior makes them feel loved, then it is important to practice that when you are around them. That is their love language. We all have behaviors that may be different from others that make us feel loved and valued.

2. **COMPLIMENTS**: A simple compliment gives you or your family member a sense of value. Being told that they are doing a good job when they are working is all the encouragement they need. It puts a smile on their face and makes them feel valued. If someone appreciates

compliments, they are more likely to give compliments. It is a simple way to show caring about another person.

3. **GIFTS**: Gifts are your way of showing how much you care. Spending time to find the special gift gives you great pleasure. I'm not talking about just big gifts here. A crayoned picture made by your child is priceless! That is their way of showing how much they love you. If gifts are important to a person, then they really appreciate your spending time finding a special gift for them.

4. **ACTS OF SERVICE**: Helping someone by mowing their lawn, babysitting, running an errand, or helping a friend in any way big or small, makes YOU feel good. I have always thought that the nice feeling you get in your gut after doing something nice for someone is the Universe's way of saying thank you. It is your way of showing you care and it makes you feel good.

5. **QUALITY TIME**: Children and families love this one. They want to spend time with you and do things with you. They need your attention and feel abandoned and unloved when you are never around. Being isolated is very hard on most people. When you spend time with people you show that they are important to you.

If you look at these five behaviors, you may see some of yourself in one or more of them. These are five common ones, but by no means ALL of them.

What do you do if your family or friends don't speak YOUR language and you don't speak theirs? Change YOUR behavior. We can't change anyone but OURSELVES. If you are having problems getting along with someone, pay attention to what they do and see if you can determine THEIR language. Then try speaking it through YOUR actions.

As you start to speak someone's language, they start to feel valued and have a more positive response. It may take longer than you expected to rebuild a relationship. It's unfair to expect too much of people who have been hurt from years of your addictive behavior.

For example:

- If you like quality time but your mate likes compliments, maybe you could try giving them compliments, even if compliments are not important to you. It may take them a while to see the shift in your behavior. Be aware that doing something a few times to get what you want is NOT what I'm talking about.
- It may be that you like compliments, but your mate likes acts of service. Try taking out the garbage or offer to run an errand. That speaks volumes!

As you start to speak someone's language, they start to feel appreciated and respond better. Remember, you can only change YOUR behavior. It may take longer than you expect to rebuild a relationship.

Most people need to improve their communication skills. When you leave "WHAT ABOUT ME" out of your vocabulary and move to "WHAT ABOUT YOU," you open up a door and start to improve your communication.

The first thing about learning a new language is that we have to learn a little of someone else's language (whether it is verbal or physical) to communicate. If you want to learn someone else's love language, watch what they do. Most people do what they like.

- If you like compliments, you usually give them.
- If you like helping others, you are a natural helper and don't have to be asked.
- If you like physical touch, you show caring with touch.
- You spend time with people you care about if quality time is important to you.
- If gifts are important to you, you show your love through gifts.

Look to see what they do routinely and try to use "their language" to communicate.

Before we end the subject on COMMUNICATION, there is one more area that should be mentioned.

CONFLICT RESOLUTION

Before you respond in anger when you are upset, ask yourself these four questions.

1. Does it NEED to be said? Or do you just WANT to say it.
2. Does it NEED to be said by YOU? Or maybe you're not the person to tell them.
3. Does it NEED to be said NOW? Or can it wait until a better time.
4. Can you say it in a CARING WAY?

If you say NO to ANY of the four questions, SAY NOTHING!! You will be amazed how the conflict in your life will start to decrease.

Remember that learning any new skill takes a lot of practice, just like riding that bike. Developing a new language requires practice. Study it in others and use it to communicate.

Be the change
You want to see in others

Mahatma Gandhi

UNFORGIVING

Forgiveness is hard for everyone. We all have trouble forgiving others for things they may have done to us. It is even harder to forgive ourselves for things we have done.

The story below is true. It was a sermon given by Reverend Jimmy Only and he graciously gave me a copy. I have edited parts of the story.

"Forgiving the Unforgivable"

Mary's heart was broken, shattered into a million pieces. Her beloved son was dead, a victim of senseless violence. But this Mary's son was not named Jesus. His name was Laramium Byrd and he didn't die on the cross 2000 years ago. He was shot to death at a party after an argument escalated into violence. He was 20 years old. His mother, Mary Johnson, had to be restrained in court, her anger boiling over. Staring at her son's killer, she saw nothing more than a cold blooded animal that deserved to be caged.

The killer who pulled the gun and shot Mary's son twice in the chest and once between the eyes was a 16 year old kid named O'Shea Israel. O'Shea lived a double life. His high school teachers knew him as a well-respected participant in the school's peer to peer conflict resolution program. Outside of the school walls, O'Shea's life descended into the dead-end cycle of drugs and gangs. Having no priors, but being tried as an adult, O'Shea was convicted of second degree murder and sentenced to 25 years in prison.

It could have ended right there and most times it does. Most of the time the victim's family sinks into the quicksand of pain, anger, and hate. For a time, Mary lost herself in the grief and bitterness of a parent who buried her only child. TWELVE YEARS passed and Mary found that she could no longer live with all the anger and hate.

Mary knew she needed to talk to her son's killer. For a time O'Shea refused her repeated requests. Finally, he decided that since he had killed her son, the least he could do was hear what she had to say.

In a National Public Radio interview, Mary Johnson and O'Shea Israel recalled that first meeting.

"I wanted to know if you were in the same mindset of what I remembered in court, where I wanted to go over and hurt you," Mary tells O'Shea. "But you were not that 16 year old. You were a grown man. I shared with you about my son."

"And he became human to me," O'Shea said.

At the end of their meeting at the prison, Mary was overcome by emotion. "The initial thing to do was just try and hold you up as best I could," O'Shea said. "I just hugged you like I would my mother."

Mary said "after you left the room, I began to say I just hugged the man that murdered my son. I knew that all that anger and animosity, all the stuff I had in my heart for twelve years for you was gone. I had totally forgiven you." Mary's forgiveness has brought both changes and challenges to O'Shea's life.

"Sometimes I still don't know how to take it," O'Shea said, "because I haven't forgiven myself yet. It is something I am learning, it's a process that I'm going through."

"I treat you as I would treat my son," Mary said, "and our relationship is beyond belief."

We all have trouble forgiving others for things they may have done to us. It is even harder to forgive ourselves for things we have done.

What motivated Mary to forgive O'Shea? Mary NEEDED to forgive O'Shea for her own sake.

She said, "UNFORGIVING is like cancer…it will eat you from the inside out. It's not about the other person. My forgiving him does not diminish what he's done. Yes, he murdered my son. But the forgiveness is for me. It's for me." Had she not forgiven O'Shea, Mary would have spent the rest of her life consumed by grief and anger. For her own sake, for her own mental and emotional wellbeing, Mary forgave O'Shea.

FORGIVING makes a new life possible. FORGIVING is NOT easy. It is HARD.

Do not think for a moment that this process for Mary happened quickly. It took her twelve years to see O'Shea. She says, "No question that it takes time for a hurting parent to get to that place of forgiveness. By that forgiveness I have been set free from anger and bitterness."

When you forgive, it does not always feel warm and fuzzy. And you may never feel that way. But it allows you to let go of the negative feelings that will destroy you.

The Chair and Unforgiving

What happens when you hold on to anger, revenge, worthlessness, and all the other negative feelings that keep you from having a good life?

Many times YOU are the one who pays the price, NOT the person who hurt you. They may go through their entire life not thinking about you at all.

Let's put it in context of picking up a LARGE CHAIR (which represents your UNFORGIVING). You carry around this CHAIR into all daily functions. Think about having relationships with your family and the CHAIR keeps getting in the way. You can't sit and play with your children if you are full of resentment or anger. They sense those feelings from you even if they don't understand what is causing it.

Many families are destroyed because the focus is on UNFORGIVING instead of loving each other. Something as simple as getting on a bus and aggravating people by bumping into them (with your invisible chair full of UNFORGIVING) causes conflict. When people have a bad response, we are shocked and react with anger. Why are they being rude when all I am doing is trying to get on the bus and find a seat?

You are the last person to figure out that carrying that CHAIR represents all your UNFORGIVING.

Would you be a good employee if you walked into your job (with your chair of UNFORGIVING) and caused constant chaos? It is even harder when you don't think the problem is you, but everyone else does. Getting fired turns into a pattern.

When you carry the CHAIR to bed with you, intimate relations with someone you care for are almost impossible. It gets very crowded in that bed when you continue to focus on rejection and negativity. It's always someone else's fault.

In some cases, you think you hurt someone so badly that you don't deserve to be forgiven. Maybe you ruined a life or lives with your actions and can't repair the damage that you caused. Making amends is a place to start, if that's possible. Many times that is not the case, but continuing to destroy your life with drugs or alcohol is not the answer.

People try to get rid of uncomfortable feelings with alcohol or drugs. That does not work. You are still carrying the CHAIR and it keeps getting heavier. You add all the problems of losing control of your life and turn it over to the drug.

THERE IS ANOTHER WAY!! Put down the CHAIR. How do you do that?

Making any change is uncomfortable at first. Something as simple as putting your watch on your other wrist or parting your hair differently doesn't feel right. You get comfortable with what you know even if it is slowly destroying you.

Learning anything new takes practice and effort. It is not accomplished in one day. It takes a lot of practice to change, but just like riding that bike, it also gives you a new freedom.

Let's start with some simple steps:

- **Stop talking about it.** Stop talking about your past drama to everyone. That's very hard to do initially, but it will get easier. You will begin to realize how much of your time is spent rehashing the drama and keeps your UNFORGIVING alive.

- **Stop inflicting wounds.** Stop giving yourself permission to continue to hurt yourself or others due to something that happened in the past. We can only change our future, not our past.

- **Stop meditating on it.** When we focus on a thought it grows bigger. Much of your time is spent reliving your past and reliving the anger and resentment or uncomfortable feelings. You feel trapped in this dead-end cycle. Replace those negative thoughts with a positive thought.

- **Use a mantra.** Find a word or thought that inspires you and keep repeating it OUT LOUD. It is impossible for the brain to think about something when it is saying something else OUT LOUD at the same time. Try singing your ABC's out loud and concentrate on some negative thought at the same time. You can't. Remember, WORDS ARE CONTAINERS OF POWER. What you say has tremendous power over how you feel.

- **Start doing something physical.** Walk, run, clean (that might be a little extreme). Just get moving. It naturally increases the "feel good" endorphins, like Dopamine, in your body.

- **Make a gratitude list.** Write down five things you are grateful for EVERY day. That is a BIG STEP! It changes your focus.

You will get better every day. When you stop focusing on all the things on the CHAIR, you will be able to gently discard all the things that you have allowed to define you. You are worth so much more than a CHAIR full of UNFORGIVING.

MAKE ONE POSITIVE CHANGE IN YOUR LIFE TODAY.

WHEN BAD THINGS HAPPEN
IT CAN CHANGE YOU
IT CAN DESTROY YOU
IT CAN MAKE YOU STRONGER
YOUR CHOICE

(Anonymous)

Diane Deeley RN, C.A.R.N.

THE COLD WITHIN

Six humans trapped by happenstance
In dark and bitter cold
Each one possessed a stick of wood
Or so the story's told.

Their dying fire in need of logs
One woman held hers back
For on the faces around the fire
She noticed one was black.

The next one looking across the way
Saw one not of his church
And couldn't bring himself to give
The fire his stick of birch.

The third one sat in tattered clothes
And gave his coat a hitch —
"Why should my log be used
to aid the idle rich?"

The rich man just sat back and thought
Of the wealth he had in store
And how to keep what he had earned
From the lazy, shiftless poor.

The black man's face bespoke revenge
As the fire passed from his sight
For all he saw in his stick of wood
Was a chance to spite the white.

The last man in this forlorn group
Did not except for gain
Giving only to those who gave
Was how he played the game.

Six logs held tight in death's still hands
Was proof of human sin
They didn't die from the cold without
They died from the cold within

Author unknown

REACT VS. RESPOND

When we focus on something (anything) we give it more power. If you shine a flashlight on something, it takes your attention to that area. Many times, we shine our "flashlight" on things that scare us, or worry us, or makes us afraid or angry. As we concentrate on these things, they grow larger in our mind. We start thinking more and more about those uncomfortable feelings. Many people find they must react to these uncomfortable feelings immediately. They make an instant bad decision and it usually has a bad consequence.

It may help to explain what is happening in the body when you are under stress.

There is a small area in the mid-brain called the **Amygdala**. It reacts instantly with an EMOTIONAL response such as fear or anger. No thinking involved. It tells the body to release stress hormones for an immediate response. During the time of the cavemen it helped them respond instantly to danger, to outrun the lion or use their strength to protect themselves. Today we know that those stress hormones also affect our body with high blood pressure, heart disease, stomach problems, obesity, asthma, diabetes, depression, anxiety, etc.

There is another area of the brain called the **Prefrontal Cortex**. This part of the brain can slow down the **Amygdala's** instant reaction and let some thinking enter into the situation. You may not even be aware of what is causing your anger or fear because it happens so quickly. It's important to know that the **Amygdala's** response is INSTANT, but it takes the **Prefrontal Cortex** about ten seconds to shut down the **Amygdala.**

During a stressful event, it's important to distract yourself. It gives these two brain regions time to communicate so you can respond without losing control. Take three slow deep breaths or remember the ten second rule – do not allow yourself to react instantly, but teach yourself to respond only after ten seconds. That gives your brain a chance to think clearly. The sudden rush of raw emotion is very strong.

Road rage is a good example. When someone is cut off in their car, the **Amygdala** instantly activates stress hormones. Many times law abiding citizens react with irrational behavior and hurt the other driver before rational thinking kicks in. They are REACTING, not RESPONDING.

Once you start REACTING, the feelings get more intense and the anger, pain, fear, worry, and desire for your drug intensifies. Learning to distract yourself takes practice.

Focus on the small things that make you happy and distract yourself from negativity or cravings. Keep practicing. You can't expect to do it once and be good at it.

Stop rehashing every negative feeling or desire for a drug. Come up with a positive statement, or your Mantra, that you can say over and over.

Example: I am better than this, or, I have a family that I love.

In addition, let's focus your attention on HAPPINESS. We think that it is a feeling or place we want to get to. We can refocus our emotions on HAPPINESS. If we make that a very intense feeling, we are distracted from all other feelings.

Example: You fall in the water and can't swim. Your entire focus is on not drowning. You can't get a breath. Your lungs feel like they will burst. You are not worried about not having enough money, feeling bad about yourself, or want a drink or drug. Your focus is simply on survival. When you are finally pulled out of the water, you are so happy and grateful to breathe again. That is real HAPPINESS.

We know that when we react quickly without thinking, we make bad choices. Now we need to learn how to respond.

Learning to Respond

- MEDITATE. It is a great way to retrain yourself to respond. Focus on breathing in and out and let thoughts quietly come and go. Bring your thinking into THIS MINUTE. There are many free meditation APPS on your phone, starting with only three minutes.
- EXERCISE. Increases the feel good chemical Dopamine in your body and makes you naturally feel better.
- AVOID COMPLAINERS. Surround yourself with people who are grateful.
- SPEAK POSITIVE WORDS. Avoid negativity. That is a hard habit to break, but it is just a habit.
- GRATITUDE LIST. Change your focus to four things you are grateful for today: feeling safe, a bed, food, and someone who cares. Gratitude is a necessary tool to a happy life.

If you want to change a habit, you have to practice over and over until you do it without thinking. It develops your character and will become more comfortable every day.

LESSON: Learn to take three deep breaths before reacting. You will make a better response.

WILDERNESS JOURNEY

Sometimes a story helps us see ourselves more clearly, and we remember it better. This story starts in Egypt where Moses rescued the Israelites from exile and took them to the Promised Land. It is actually a story of RECOVERY.

The Israelites were treated as slaves. They were beaten, had no freedom, held as prisoners, and made to work on rock piles. Do you think people with addictions are like the slaves in Egypt? Held hostage to their disease? Do you feel hopeless, helpless, and not able to escape? Your free-will is taken away and you hate what your life is becoming. You don't know how to change it. Many have lost family, jobs, self-respect, or freedom, and are left with little hope that things will change. Some can relate to that hopeless feeling, but are too afraid to try to make changes or don't have a clue what to do. They stay in a terrible situation because they feel so powerless.

In the story, Moses was told by God to lead the Israelites through the Wilderness to the Promised Land. Moses had no special abilities, didn't know the way, had a speech impediment, was a murderer, and afraid. He said NO. What kind of hero was he? Maybe God knew something he didn't know. On the surface, Moses didn't appear to be the right person for the job. God told him that he would give him all the help he needed. Eventually, Moses agreed to do it and went to tell the Israelites. They thought he was nuts. It took Moses a while to convince the Israelites to follow him and many chose not to go. They were afraid and didn't trust him. Only some of the Israelites were brave enough to start the journey with Moses.

As the journey started, they had to go around mountains and through deserts and valleys. Many were frightened, tired, and complaining constantly. (Sounds like recovery to me.) They were convinced they would die in the desert. Some even went back to Egypt.

- Have you ever had a person give you a suggestion and you refused to listen because they didn't look or act like they knew anything? You may have missed a wonderful opportunity.

- If someone came to you and said "I'm not sure of the way, but God told me to lead you out of here to the Promised Land," would you stay right where you were?
- Would you think he was crazy and send him on his way? Many people stayed behind due to fear and not knowing what would happen.

When I asked our class how many would take the chance, to come to the front of the room and take the journey to the Promised Land, only a few said they would. They felt they had to do WHATEVER IT TOOK to change their lives. They didn't care if anyone laughed at them. Many others remained in their seats, because they didn't know what was to be asked of them, and didn't want to be embarrassed. That is probably close to what happens in real life.

In class we used chairs to represent the mountains and each mountain represented a character defect that needed to change. Everyone had to pick a mountain that represented their character defect and walk around the chair continuously until told to stop or develop a plan to change. Many admitted to being on the SAME mountain for years, and never realizing how long it had been. In the class demonstration, people complained of being too tired. Some gave up and went back to their seats.

Now, if Moses had a GPS, the Israelites would have made the trip in about eleven days. It took them forty years!!! Seems like a lot of wrong turns, but maybe not. Maybe the people had to go around mountains and through deserts or get lost enough until they learned to TRUST, or they finally went around their personal mountains enough to finally leave their old negative behaviors behind. We all have mountains, deserts, and valleys that we have traveled for years, not willing to give up a behavior or belief that brings us back to old habits. In this case, it is Addiction.

The mountains represent anger, fear, abuse, no self-worth, entitlement, and unforgiving. You can fill in what is on your mountain. Each one represents a character flaw that interferes with your life. The really hard part is there are so many mountains. When you finally conquer one, there are still more to climb. Moses continued to encourage the Israelites, but they didn't think he knew what he was doing. They did not TRUST that God would help them. Some people turned to go back to Egypt, which represents old behaviors.

A few common mountains include:

- I have always been smarter than all these people
- I still have a job so I'm okay
- This is way too hard
- I'm too old to change
- My whole family is like this
- I don't trust that there really is a Higher Power
- There is no hope for me
- I was abused and am too damaged
- I want it, but I'm not willing to make so many changes
- I don't deserve it because I've done some terrible things

You have to make your own list. Everyone is different. No matter what is on your list, you CAN make changes if you are willing to work on it. Practice these changes until they are part of you. Doing it once is only the start. It's like riding that bike. It takes lots of practice.

There will be a lot of grumbling and complaining as you slowly reinvent yourself. During the journey through the desert not everyone continued on. Some returned to their old ways due to fear, anger, and hopelessness. Others got lost in the journey, got lazy and didn't want to work hard, while others died in the wilderness.

When the people finally reached the Promised Land (a new sober life) many were afraid. For the ones who entered, it represents a new life, but the journey isn't over. Standing still and saying I made it isn't enough. It's important to reach out to others and help them along the way. The saying is:

YOU CAN'T KEEP IT IF YOU WON'T GIVE IT AWAY.

Recovery is a lifelong process of saying and doing the right thing even when you don't feel like it or nobody is looking. The good news is as your habit and attitudes improve, your life improves. You are becoming a person of CHARACTER.

CHANGE IS ALWAYS HARD, AND FEAR OF THE UNKNOWN IS EVEN HARDER.

SETTING BOUNDARIES

Why are boundaries important? Take a minute to think about what they do for you.

- They keep you safe and protect what belongs to you
- They give you guidelines for acceptable behavior
- They establish norms for society

Has addiction affected your boundaries? Ask yourself how and why. Do boundaries affect your personal life? What do healthy personal boundaries look like to you?

If a balloon is not inflated enough, it has no purpose. It just sits there. It represents people with no boundaries. It is flexible, but has no useful purpose. It is usually discarded in the trash.

When inflated correctly, a balloon is attractive and has a little give and take when touched. It has good healthy boundaries. Others admire it and enjoy it.

If it is overinflated, it is ridged and the slightest touch will pop it easily.

Our boundaries have to be healthy so they serve us well. We need to constantly reevaluate them.

Healthy boundaries give you a feeling of security and a better sense of who you are and what you can expect of yourself and others. You know what you are capable of doing and areas where you need improvement. You learn to function independently but also work well with others. That is why it is important to not become too rigid in your boundaries. You push others away when you always want your way. Flexibility is key.

CO-DEPENDENCE

CO-DEPENDENCE: BEING DEPENDENT ON SOMEONE OR SOMETHING FOR YOUR SELF- WORTH

Little children are totally dependent on their parents. They could not live on their own. That is normal. As they learn to dress and feed themselves, they start to become more independent. They grow up and have ideas of their own. That is healthy.

HEALTHY RELATIONSHIPS: There are parts of you that you SHARE with your family, children, and friends. But, you still have your OWN interests, hobbies, friends, jobs, etc. apart from another person. All these things make up a relationship. If the relationship ends because of separation or death, you still have enough of yourself to rebuild your life.

CO-DEPENDENCE: You change your boundaries constantly to maintain a relationship with someone or something, even if you know that it is an unhealthy relationship. You feel inadequate by yourself. You convince yourself that you can't live without this person. You constantly change what you are doing to keep someone else happy to maintain the relationship.

Two people become so intertwined that neither one can function without the other one. We all need to develop a part of ourselves to stand independently. We all enjoy being part of a "united relationship." However, you don't want to lose who you are as an individual. It is important to maintain part of yourself apart from another person.

When people are co-dependent, they feel as if nothing is left when the other person leaves due to separation or death. They have a very hard time rebuilding themselves and are very susceptible to relapse.

Many times when someone is CO-DEPENDENT, they look for another CO-DEPENDENT relationship. They are not aware that they are doing that, but gravitate towards a behavior they are comfortable with, even if it is unhealthy. It is recommended that you don't get involved in a serious relationship in early recovery. It really is a helpful idea to work on yourself and develop some healthy boundaries and ways of coping before you get involved with someone else. If you don't feel good about yourself, you are not going to look for people who are healthy. You are going to look for people who are going to buy into your CO-DEPENDENT behaviors. Once you have started to really look at your behaviors and start developing healthy coping skills, you will not try to find someone who likes you better when you were using your drugs.

I have seen people try to find someone to distract themselves from having to do the hard work of making changes while in early recovery. Unfortunately, too many times they both end up relapsing. They try to convince themselves that they will help each other but they don't have enough healthy coping skills to help themselves much less someone else.

Know that EVERYONE already has EVERYTHING they need inside themselves to live a full, productive life. It's a question of finding it and using it enough, until you are comfortable standing on your own.

HEALTHY PEOPLE ARE ATTRACTED TO HEALTHY PEOPLE

DYSFUNCTIONAL FAMILIES

Very few people are brought up in the perfect family, even if it looks like that from the outside. We all have faults. In some families, parents or caregivers may be unable to provide healthy care, possibly due to their own addictions or other issues that are unhealthy.

Many times the children in these dysfunctional families develop similar behavior patterns.

- **HERO CHILD**. The child who has to be more like the "grown up" at a very young age. You help younger brothers and sisters get ready for school, pack lunches, and take charge when the parent can't. You are responsible for doing many things and take on the parenting role.

    Question: Do you think you may have some problems taking suggestions while starting your journey of recovery? It's hard when you have been making decisions for your family since you were very young.

Lesson to Learn: ASK FOR HELP. Allow others help you.

- **SCAPEGOAT CHILD**. The child who is blamed for everything that goes wrong even if it is not your fault. You are always in trouble and become comfortable in that role. Parents don't have to look at their own issues when they are constantly blaming you for their problems.

  Question: Since you are comfortable being in trouble, do you think you may have issues believing that you can be successful in recovery?

  Lesson to Learn: Learn to accept approval and not to be afraid of SUCCESS.

- **LOST CHILD**. The child who stays "invisible" to avoid the family drama. You follow rules and draw no attention to yourself. You don't stand up for yourself.

  Question: Do you stay invisible and don't ask for help? Are you afraid you are not worth it?

  Lesson to Learn: Stand up for yourself and know that you are important in this world.

- **CLOWN CHILD**: You may use your humor and antics to deflect the fallout from the anger and craziness in the family. Many comedians admit to being a clown child.

Question: Do you continue to use your clowning behavior to protect yourself from seriously looking at behaviors that need to change?

Lesson to Learn: Take some time to look at who you really are. You are more than a funny clown.

It's important to know that many things from your past may affect how you see yourself. But it doesn't give you permission to stay stuck and do nothing. It just means you will have a better understanding of why you feel a certain way.

WITHDRAWAL

WITHDRAWAL. When you stop using a drink or drug after prolonged use, there is a period of withdrawal. It is a physical response that the body has when the drug is withdrawn. Depending on the drug, it can last for a few days to several weeks. It is very uncomfortable mentally and physically and puts the body in danger.

POST ACUTE WITHDRAWAL. After the acute physical phase is over, emotions are VERY unstable: I love this place; I hate everyone; I'm so grateful I'm clean today; I am leaving treatment; I had a good night's sleep; my tooth hurts and they won't let me go to the dentist.

These extreme mood swings are all part of Post-Acute Withdrawal syndrome or PAWS. Your mind, body, and emotions are trying to stabilize. You are at high risk to relapse because you feel so miserable, and know that a drink or drug will relieve that if only for the moment.

Dopamine is a feel good chemical. When something makes you feel good, the brain cells that make Dopamine sends a message to other brain cells. Dopamine attaches to the receptors on these cells and tells you to feel happy. After a while, some of the Dopamine goes back to the cell it came from and waits for another message.

When a drug such as Heroin hijacks that system, it fills all the receptors and makes you feel ridiculously happy. The only problem is the production of Dopamine shuts down because it hasn't been needed. The receptors sites get broken due to the rapid influx of Heroin. When you stop using Heroin, there is no Dopamine response. The receptor sites are broken so there is nothing to make you feel good. It may take a few months or up to two years for the receptors to repair themselves. This varies from person to person.

The only reason you need to know this is that you have to be extra vigilant and protect your sobriety during this time. You are doing all the right things (meetings, 12 steps work, sponsors, and staying away from people that trigger a relapse). However, you still have strong urges to use your drug. You think if you use it "just this once" and stay with the program, you will feel better. What you don't understand is you undo the healing that is occurring and go back to square one. It takes very little time for all the healing that has occurred to disappear.

TWO THINGS TO REMEMBER

- STAY SAFE DURING THIS TIME OF HEALING.
  If you decide to visit your drug dealer or hang out
  in bars or resume friendships with people you used
  with, you are probably not going to stay sober. This
  is a VERY DANGEROUS time for you. The body is
  screaming and you are feeling terrible.
- YOU ARE ALSO AT A VERY HIGH RISK OF
  OVERDOSE. If you haven't used for a few weeks or
  months, your body can't handle it. Your tolerance has
  decreased. It is so very sad that many men and women
  think they will somehow not succumb to a overdose.
  You leave treatment and think you can still do it your
  way. You go back to using and your body can't handle
  as much and you overdose. We are in the midst of losing
  so many people who have much to offer this world, but
  are dying in alarming numbers from Heroin overdoses.
  What people don't realize is that Heroin suppresses
  respirations and you stop breathing. Another factor to
  remember is many drugs have other chemicals added
  to them which increase the overdose risk.

It does take time for the body to restart manufacturing
Dopamine and repair receptor sites. Use this time to practice
positive changes you need in your life. Getting healthy in
Mind, Body and Spirit is a process and takes effort to maintain
that healthy lifestyle.

When I ask the class what they think will naturally increase Dopamine, it's amazing how many people think it is eating or sleeping. Nope! There are four ways that the body can NATURALLY stimulate the production of Dopamine.

- LAUGHING. Listen to a good joke or make yourself laugh out loud. It's amazing how good you can feel.
- CRYING. It's sad that in Western culture, crying is not encouraged. It actually does a lot of good in releasing tension, lowering blood pressure, along with relieving all kinds of stress. Stress ages us and is a cause of many diseases that are common in our fast-paced lives.
- SEX. The feel good chemical Dopamine increases during sex.
- EXERCISE. Taking a walk, jog, swim, or any physical exercise makes you feel better and relieves stress.

Recovery is a process. It takes time. If you break a leg, the doctor has to put it in a cast and let the bones heal. You can't do a lot of things during that time and it is uncomfortable and limiting. But you can't rush it or it won't heal correctly.

Recovery is also a slow, annoying process, but when you work at it, you get your life back and your freedom increases.

HOW TO SPOT A RELAPSE

People always tell me that the relapse "just happened" after some EVENT, such as:

- Job loss
- Relationship issues
- Financial problems
- Loneliness
- Arguments

RELAPSE PROCESS: Relapse starts quite a while before picking up the drink or drug. It can start several weeks, months, or even years before. The good news is that it typically starts with changes in behavior. These changes in behavior are very similar each time for each individual. This means that YOUR behaviors and emotions will be the same with YOUR relapse, even if the final event that was the last straw is different.

At this point you have discarded all your protective armor. The feelings are so uncomfortable that you feel powerless over them. You know that your drug of choice will relieve those uncomfortable feelings, if only for a moment.

If you really want to stay sober, then you are going to have to take an honest look at your behaviors on a daily basis. Sound excessive? So is your addiction!

TRACKING A RELAPSE

We had a volunteer in class track his relapse. We will call him Joe. Joe said he was sober for six-and-a-half years and then relapsed. He was mystified how it happened since he thought he was doing well up until the day of his relapse. Let's take a closer look at Joe's behaviors.

YEAR ONE: After starting his sobriety journey, Joe was going to meetings almost daily, had a sponsor and talked to him about many issues. Joe was working, surrounded by sober friends, and living with family. He was happy with his life.

YEAR TWO: Joe was basically doing the same things. Life was going well.

YEAR THREE: No big changes except he started working more, but he couldn't remember why. Joe continued with his sponsor, NA meetings, and sober support network.

YEAR FOUR: Joe said nothing had changed, but he moved in with a girlfriend. He was working even more. He was not in touch as frequently with family. He still attended NA meetings, but not regularly. He had his sponsor, but did not see him as often. The girlfriend was not working, but she continued to spend money. He was becoming resentful.

YEAR FIVE: Attendance at NA meetings diminished. Not talking with his sponsor. He was working even more. (Why was he working so much?) He finally admitted his girlfriend moved out because he was cheating on her. (The honesty piece is now missing.) He moved away from his family and his sober support network.

YEAR SIX: Joe had a new girlfriend, no NA, no sponsor, and isolated from old sober friends. Resentful that all he did was work, he no longer enjoyed his life. He's starting to think he was okay because he hadn't picked up his drug of choice. Admitted to smoking POT on occasion. (Insisted he never had a problem with POT and never craved it.) He was isolating, resentful, less honest, feeling trapped, and no longer enjoyed his life.

He was becoming more discontent every day. A few months later he ran into an old friend who offered him a Percodan pill for his headache!!! That was the EVENT. He was back using Heroin the next day.

He had convinced himself that as long as he didn't actually pick up his drug of choice, he was still sober. It had never occurred to him that he had been in relapse mode for a few years and all he had to do is find an EVENT (running into someone who gave him a Percodan pill). He never realized how many behaviors he had changed.

Everyone has behaviors that are signals that they are going off track in their life. People may confront you, but many times they are pushed away. As you give up the protections you learned in recovery, you find yourself angry, afraid, alone, and desperate. These are such painful and intense feelings, and you don't think you can deal with them without a drink or drug. You promise yourself it will be just this once.

You slowly begin to get careless, start to climb BUD mountain, and start shedding protections you have learned in recovery. BUD stands for BUILDING UP TO A DRINK/DRUG. You shed your sober friends, restart negative attitudes, old behaviors start to appear, and your coping skills start to decrease. You don't notice the changes. They are usually small and don't cause a problem at first. When you get to the top of BUD mountain and have shed all your recovery tools, you have no protection. It is so uncomfortable, that any EVENT will tip you over the top and you fall off the mountain into a drink or drug to numb the pain.

COMMON RELAPSE BEHAVIORS

Here are some very common relapse behaviors that start to sneak back into your life. You need to watch for these:

- SILENT TYPE. You pull into yourself and no longer reach out to anyone who will help you process your feelings or call you on bad behaviors. You stop using any suggestions from others and do not discuss any uncomfortable feelings such as anger, hurt, fear, and resentment.

- TALKATIVE TYPE. Talking constantly and acting as if you have all the answers. Not open to suggestions and big on telling others how to live their lives.

- ANGRY. Push people away with your angry behavior. It's a defense mechanism porcupines use when they strike out their quills for protection. It's also a way to control others. Very unapproachable.

- BORED. Start talking about how boring life is now that you are not using and that you are unhappy with your life. GET OVER YOURSELF. When AA/NA gets boring, look around at meetings and find a person who looks uncomfortable. Talk to them about what early recovery is like. My friend started his recovery in prison by asking God to help him. In return, he would stop his drugs (he used them all) and devote his life to helping others. I met him in Africa on a medical mission ship. He was working as a machinist. He was a big guy, 6'5" tall and probably the gentlest and kindest person on the ship. His life isn't boring. He and his wife and children now run an orphanage in West Africa! Doing something for someone else quickly takes the focus off yourself and boredom seems to disappear.

- LYING. When you are using, lying protects your use and is a necessary evil. When you start lying (when you have no reason to except it's a habit), it's a sign of going back to old behaviors. Remember the **10th Step**. **Take a daily inventory and when you're wrong, promptly admit it.** Lying is not a habit you want to re-invite back into your life.

- COMPLACENCY. You no longer see any value working your program or working the 12 STEPS to change habits and improve your character. You feel healthy, things are going well. You start to think that "maybe I am cured". I don't need all this support anymore.

- FORGETTING GRATITUDE. You stop being grateful for the positive things that are back in your life. You lose sight of all the blessings that have come your way. Your health is restored or you were invited for the holidays for the first time in years.

This list may be a little different for you since everyone is different, but YOUR LIST IS THE SAME EVERY TIME. Everyone has behaviors that are signals they are going off track. People may confront you, but many times they are pushed away. As you give up the protections you have learned in recovery, you find yourself angry, afraid, alone, and desperate.

A good tool is a RELAPSE PREVENTION AGREEMENT (see a copy of the Relapse Agreement is at the end of this chapter). Give it to someone you trust enough (a parent, significant other, children, boss, sponsor, or close friend) and who is brave enough to bring to your attention the poor choices you are starting to make in your behaviors.

Give it to people when you are serious about cleaning up your life, not when you are already running up the mountain towards a relapse. If you are just starting to let go of some positive behaviors you have developed, and allowing old habits to slowly creep back into your life, it is much easier to climb down off the mountain and get back on track. The higher you climb, the less likely you will be willing to make the changes. It is also harder to be honest with yourself and to acknowledge that you are in danger.

- Family, including children, good friends, co-workers, and sponsors will notice those changes before you do. It is common to start excluding these people from your life. It is very hard for them to approach you. Many times they will keep silent and hope you are just having a bad day. Other times they may say something and

> are "shut down" by your attitude. "I'm NOT using so leave me alone".
>
> - I believe if you really want to keep off BUD mountain, you need all the help you can find. BEFORE YOU RELAPSE, I suggest you give a relapse agreement to people who will bring it to your attention when they start to see these changes in your behavior.

EXAMPLES: Lying, less reliable, angry, withdrawn or whatever behaviors raise a red flag that you need to make changes.

Once you start to recognize your patterns of relapse, you will be able to make changes and get back on track before you actually start using again. You start developing your character and start liking yourself more.

RELAPSE AGREEMENT CONTRACT

I_____

give_____

My permission to bring to my attention changes in my behaviors
listed below

1. _____
2. _____
3. _____
4. _____
5. _____

Sign _____

Date_____

BUILDING YOUR SUPPORTS

HOUSING:

When you are deciding on where you are going after treatment, ask yourself a few questions about where you will live.

- Will you be alone or live with a sober friend or family member?
- Is it safe there with no one using any drink or drug?
- What are the rules in the house?
- No using or selling drugs by anyone?

Sometimes it is recommended that you go to a halfway house or long term treatment. Many people resist it and want to go home. Unfortunately, many people haven't built a sober support network yet, and don't have enough safe contacts. They feel isolated on their own and are in danger of relapse. Try using **Step Three. Make a decision to turn our will and our**

lives over to the care of God as we understood him. You need to accept help from others even when you don't want to.

FAMILY:

Will you have to keep a distance from family (if they are using)? Do you expect them to support you?

Family members may have problems with trust issues towards you. Expect it. If your behavior has affected them in a negative way, don't expect too much from them. It takes time to rebuild their trust. You've said SORRY many times, but SORRY means nothing without a change in your behavior.

FRIENDS:

Will you have to eliminate being around some people due to their continued use? It is hard to walk away from old friends, but they are dangerous to be around even if they are not using, but are selling drugs. It's important to set clear boundaries with some people to stay safe. Don't expect too much of people you have hurt. Trust is something you earn.

AA FRIENDS:

It's important to build a sober network of people. You need people to talk to and who will listen and offer advice when needed. Surround yourself with positive people who are really working on improving their life. People who are just "talking the talk" but not changing are toxic for you. People who are negative and always complaining or angry and disruptive will not encourage your sobriety.

Maybe this story will help you realize how powerful AA friends can be.

I never forgot the man who arrived in our drug rehab, and everything he owned was contained in a small plastic bag from a grocery store. He was born on the island of Jamaica and at some point he moved to NYC. I am not sure how he ended up in rehab in upstate NY that day.

He was about 30 years old. During the week he arrived, we had four other men that were also admitted. They had not known each other before coming to the rehab.

The four men and Juan (not his real name) bonded instantly and spent a lot of time talking and eating together. They formed quite a bond in the 28 days they were at the rehab. The men were older than Juan and all had good jobs. Juan had never had the opportunity to get his high school education.

Fast forward nine or ten years. I was working as a nurse in Albany. Juan startled me when he first approached me. I didn't recognize him. His story was amazing. He said that he had never relapsed and had gotten his GED and then his Associates degree from a local college. He then continued his education with a scholarship to another college and had just received his Masters!

He had come a long way. I asked about the other four men and if he ever saw them. He replied, "Oh yes, we still have coffee once a week and keep each other sober. They were a big part of my going back to school."

His story is proof that IT WORKS IF YOU WORK IT.

SPONSOR:

What is a sponsor? It is someone with some good sobriety who is willing to share what they have learned and be a good support for you. Good sobriety means they continue to work their own program and not just talking the talk. They have a positive outlook and are enjoying life. Look for someone who is sober, not just dry. Part of the program of AA or NA is passing it along to help others.

It is important to have a connection with a person who you can talk over issues with and will call you on behaviors that you need to change. Be sure your sponsor has not taken on more people than they can help at once. They are great support, but cannot be your only support.

You can never have too much support, especially in early recovery.

WORD FOR FAMILY AND FRIENDS

Dealing with your significant other, son, daughter, sister, brother, or another family member as they struggle with an addiction of any kind is overwhelming. You have to deal with your own feelings of thinking it is your fault, or you are angry that they are causing such havoc in everyone's life. No one is immune to the devastation that it causes. Families get broken apart and friends are lost. If you have never been addicted to anything, it is hard to understand the overwhelming pull it can have on everyone.

Unfortunately, the problem has been introduced into your life and you have to learn how to deal with it. I think the first thing you have to do is set HEALTHY BOUNDARIES for yourself. You have to figure out what your expectations are for their behavior when that person is in your presence or living with you.

The best suggestion I can give you is to go to AL ANON or NAR ANON meetings. It is for families and friends who live with or love a person with addictions. It is a fellowship of people helping each other to cope with their loved ones' addictions. Look on the computer to see which one is near you. There is no cost and you will find support from people dealing with the same issues. They will give you good ideas about what has worked for them.

Be supportive but know that YOU cannot fix this. It is up to them to make changes for a better life. You have to be strong and stick to your boundaries or you will be of no help to them or yourself. Your home has to remain a safe place for everyone. Continually bailing them out of problems or moving your boundaries will only delay them having to change.

It is hard to believe them when they say "I want recovery". It is difficult to understand that there are so many behaviors to change. It takes time to make even simple changes. Being consistent is not easy. It is a life long journey, but we all have to do it ONE DAY AT A TIME.

GOD,

GRANT ME THE

SERENITY

TO ACCEPT THE THINGS

I CANNOT CHANGE,

THE COURAGE

TO CHANGE

THE THINGS I CAN,

AND THE

WISDOM

TO KNOW THE

DIFFERENCE.

Printed in the United States
By Bookmasters